GW01376128

This sign shows you that there is an investigation you can do to find out more about the Earth.

First published 1993
A & C Black (Publishers) Limited
35 Bedford Row, London WC1R 4JH
Reprinted 1994

ISBN 0-7136-3630-0

© 1993 A & C Black (Publishers) Limited

A CIP catalogue record for this book
is available from the British Library

Acknowledgements
Illustrations by Dennis Tinkler
Photographs by Robert Pickett, except for: p2 (top) The Creative Company, Milton Keynes; pp3, 5 NASA; pp2 (bottom), 23 NASA (from Genesis Space Photo Library); pp10/11, 15 Geo Science Features Picture Library; p13 Susan Gadsby (Papilio); p18 C. Lush (Papilio).

The author and publisher would like to thank the staff and pupils of Eardley Junior School, Streatham.

All rights reserved. No part of this publication may be reproduced in any form or by any means – graphic, electronic or mechanical, including photocopying, recording, taping or information storage and retrieval systems – without the prior permission in writing of the publishers.

Filmset by Rowland Phototypesetting Limited, Bury St Edmunds, Suffolk.
Printed in Great Britain by Cambus Litho Limited, East Kilbride.

INVESTIGATING SPACE

The Earth

Anne Cohen
Photographs by Robert Pickett

Contents

Planet Earth	2
What makes the Earth special?	4
Why is the Sun so important?	6
What is gravity?	8
What is the Earth made of?	10
Investigating rocks	12
What are fossils?	14
Investigating soil	16
The Earth's water supply	18
Investigating rainfall	20
Make a weather diary	22
Notes for teachers and parents	24
Index	25

A & C Black · London

Planet Earth

The Earth is one of nine planets that are travelling round the Sun. The Earth is round like a football, but from where we live on its surface it looks flat. Even from the window of an aeroplane, it's impossible to see the curve of the Earth, because it curves so gradually.

The photograph below was taken from the Space Shuttle, high above the Earth. At this distance, the Earth's surface begins to look curved.

The Apollo space astronauts took this photograph as they looked back at Earth on their journey to the Moon. The astronauts saw that the Earth is a ball of rock, partly covered with water. Cloud patterns show up white against the blue oceans. The astronauts thought that the Earth looked beautiful and called it 'the blue planet'.

What makes the Earth special?

About four-and-a-half thousand million years ago, the Sun, the Earth and all the other planets were formed from a swirling disk of gas and dust.

As far as we know, Earth is the only place in the Solar System to have life on it. Mercury and Venus are closer than the Earth to the Sun, and are so hot that nothing can survive on them. The other planets and their moons are bitterly cold.

Earth began to form here.

The Earth is surrounded by a very thin layer of air called the atmosphere. You cannot see Earth's atmosphere because it is a mixture of invisible gases. This layer of gases is so thin compared to Earth, that if Earth were an apple, the atmosphere would be the thickness of the apple-skin.

The Sun's warmth is trapped by the gases in the atmosphere. This makes the temperature on Earth suitable for living things. The atmosphere also forms an invisible screen to protect us from the Sun's damaging ultra-violet rays and x-rays.

The flat disk spins slowly round.

The atmosphere contains oxygen. This is a gas that animals need to breathe in order to live. When this astronaut walked on the surface of the Moon, he carried on his back a supply of oxygen in a tank. There is no oxygen on the Moon, and no water, so nothing can survive on its surface. Water is vital for life.

Why is the Sun so important?

The Sun's light and heat reach us on the Earth's surface from across space. All life on Earth depends on this energy from the Sun.

Plants need the light and warmth of the Sun to feed and grow. You can test this by finding out what happens if plants are kept in the dark. Plant two pots of the same seeds in some damp soil. Cress seeds are good to use because they come up very quickly.

Keep one pot in a dark cupboard and the other on a window sill. What happens to the seeds in each pot? Can you think of a way to change the investigation to find out what happens to plants if they are not kept warm enough?

Animals too get their energy from the Sun. This iguana is using the Sun's warmth to raise its body temperature. It needs to warm up so that it can become more active.

People have learnt to use the Sun's energy to heat water for use in houses and power stations. You can see how solar energy works by putting a tray of water outdoors in a sunny place. Measure the temperature of the water at the start of the experiment and again after a couple of hours. You'll probably find that a black tray works best. Why do you think this is?

What is gravity?

Why don't we fall off the Earth as it spins and travels round the Sun? Think about what happens to your body when you jump into the air or trip over – you always drop downwards until you reach the ground. This happens because of the force of gravity, which pulls you down towards the ground.

Now think about people living in different places on the Earth. You can represent them with models stuck on to a globe. It doesn't matter where people live – whether it's in Australia, Europe, Asia or America – each person would say that 'downwards' is towards their feet. So the pull of gravity must be towards the centre of the Earth.

Can you imagine what would happen to us if there were no force of gravity to anchor us down to the Earth's surface?

When you drop something, gravity makes it fall faster and faster until it hits the ground. You can investigate the force of gravity. Try dropping two objects of different weights from exactly the same height. Do they hit the ground together? Very light objects such as feathers fall more slowly because the air drags on them and slows them down. If there were no air, feathers would hit the ground at the same time as very large weights.

What is the Earth made of?

When the Earth was formed, the heavier or denser material sank to the middle and the lighter rocks stayed near the surface. The central part of the Earth is called the core. It is solid and made of iron and nickel. Around the core is a layer of very hot liquid which is mainly made of melted iron. The temperature of this layer is about 6000°C.

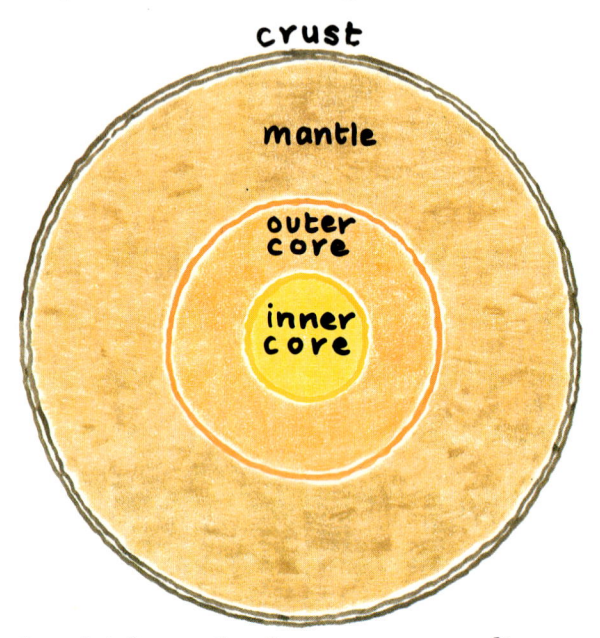

The thick, rocky layer surrounding the liquid part of the Earth's core is called the mantle. Parts of the mantle are hot enough to be molten, or liquid. Molten rock is called magma. Magma from deep in the mantle sometimes rises to the Earth's surface and is pushed out suddenly. This makes a volcano, like the one in this picture. The red hot liquid that is thrown out is called lava.

The crust, the thin top layer of the Earth, is the part that we live on. The mountains, the land around us and the sea-bed are all part of the crust.

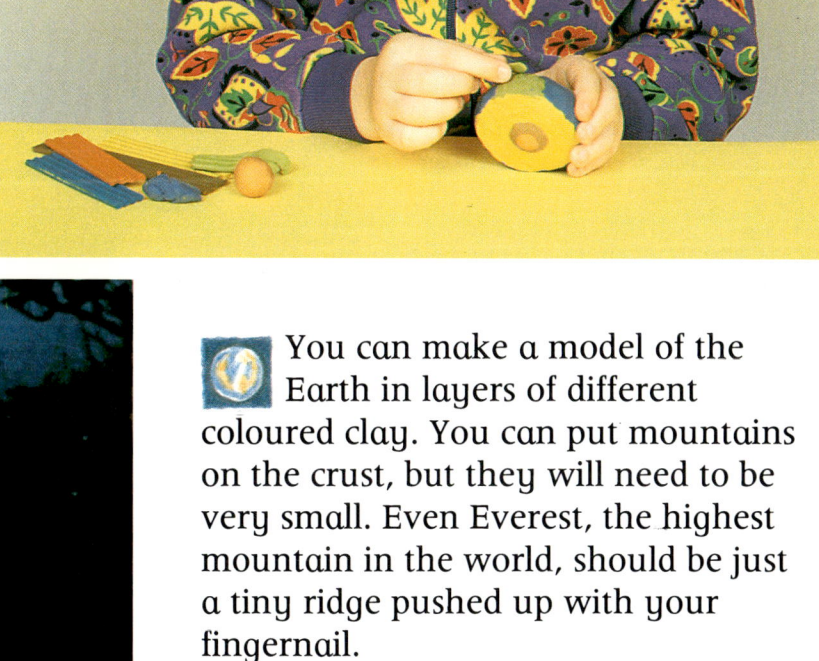

You can make a model of the Earth in layers of different coloured clay. You can put mountains on the crust, but they will need to be very small. Even Everest, the highest mountain in the world, should be just a tiny ridge pushed up with your fingernail.

Investigating rocks

The Earth's crust is formed of many kinds of rock. Some rocks are made from magma that has cooled slowly over millions of years. Rocks that are formed in this way contain crystals.

If the magma cooled very slowly, large crystals were made. You can see an example of this if you look at a piece of granite, which is often speckled with crystals made of different substances. Perhaps you've seen gemstone jewellery which is made from precious crystals.

You can see how crystals are made by making your own. Dissolve half a cupful of salt in a dish of hot water. Pour some of the mixture on to a saucer and let it cool slowly and dry up. Crystals of salt will form in the bottom of the saucer.

Choose one of the largest crystals and hang it from a thread of cotton. Dangle the crystal you've made in a jar containing some very salty water. The crystal will take weeks to grow bigger, so be patient. Don't move the jar!

See if you can find some rocks which contain crystals. Beaches are a good place to look for pebbles and rocks that have crystals in them.

What are fossils?

The beach is also a good place to look for another sort of rock which is made under the sea or in river beds. Over millions of years, sand and soil settled in layers at the bottom of seas and rivers. Dead plants and animals were buried in these layers.

As the layers hardened, the plants and animals were left in the rock. The harder parts of the plants and animals, such as stems, bones and shells, did not rot away but gradually turned to stone to form fossils.

Fossils can tell us a lot about life on Earth millions of years ago. This is a fossil of a reptile that lived about 150 million years ago. We can tell the age of the fossil from the type of rock in which it was found.

You can look for fossils in quarries or in cliffs at the seaside. The land that now forms some of the cliffs and quarries lay on sea and river beds before being pushed to the surface over millions of years. You can often see the layers in the rock.

Take care when you explore cliffs and quarries – always take an adult with you. Also, you can find out whether your local museum has a collection of fossils that people have found in your area.

Investigating soil

Soil and stones are made of broken up rock. It may be difficult for you to find bare rock in your area because it is hidden beneath roads, buildings or fields. But you can easily find soil in gardens, parks or fields.

sand

grit

humus

clay

chalk

There are many different types of soil and they vary from place to place. All soils contain different mixtures of sand, clay, grit and chalk. These are tiny pieces of rock which have been worn away from larger lumps of rock by the weather. Soils also contain humus, which is formed from the remains of dead plants and animals.

You can break down a sample of soil from your local area into its different parts. Shake up a tablespoonful of soil in a jam jar of water. Leave the mixture to settle for an hour or two.

The heaviest material such as stones and grit will settle at the bottom of the jar, with a layer of finer sand on top. If there is clay in your soil it will take days to settle and will make the water in your jar look cloudy.

You'll find bits of twigs, roots, stalks and other dead plant material floating on top of the water. This is the humus. You may also find worms and other small animals.

Try the same investigation with two or three soil samples from different places to see if there are any differences in the layers which they form.

17

The Earth's water supply

Almost three-quarters of the Earth's surface is covered with water. This is mostly salty water in the oceans and seas, and there is also frozen water at the north and south poles. The fresh water that we drink and use at home comes from rivers, lakes and streams.

All living things contain water. A lettuce is nine-tenths water. Water makes up two-thirds of your own body. Human beings can survive for much longer without food than they can without water. You can test how vital water is to plants if you try to grow two sets of cress seeds, one in damp soil and the other in dry soil.

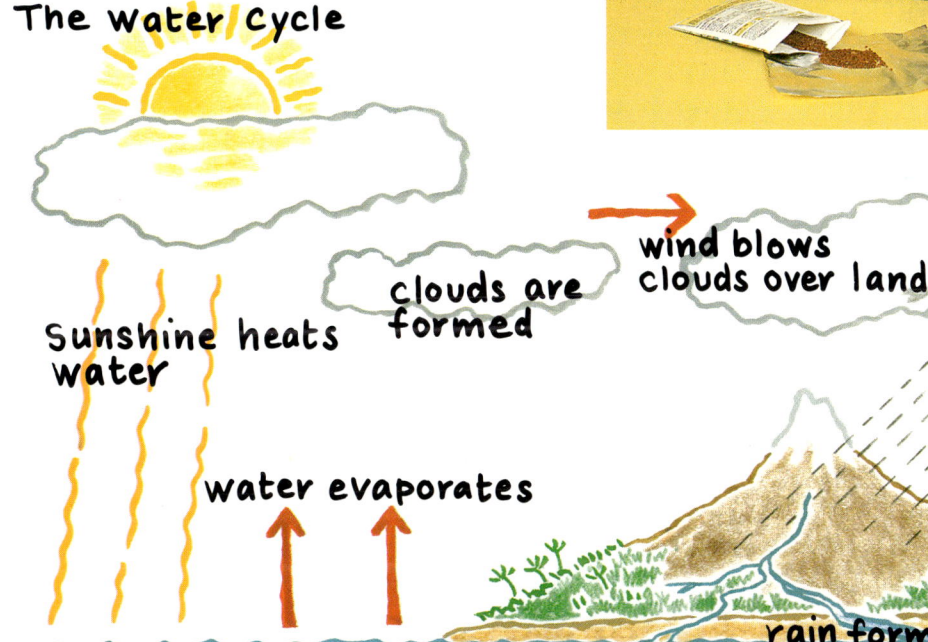

The water cycle

Sunshine heats water

water evaporates

clouds are formed

wind blows clouds over land

Clouds cool and turn into raindrops

rain forms streams and rivers which flow to the sea

Our supply of fresh water on Earth is constantly being renewed in a process called the water cycle. The Sun shines on the seas and lakes and warms the water on the surface. The Sun's heat makes some of the water evaporate, or turn to moisture in the air. This is how clouds are made.

The clouds are blown over land by the wind. The hills push the clouds higher into the sky where the air is cooler. As the clouds cool, they turn into raindrops. Rain falls to the ground and forms streams and rivers which take the water back to the lakes and seas.

19

Investigating rainfall

Measure how much rain falls each day in your local area. You can make your own rain gauge by cutting a plastic bottle in half and fitting the top half upside down in the base to form a funnel. Put your rain gauge away from buildings and wedge it with bricks to stop it blowing away.

Next morning, pour any water that has collected in the bottom of the base into a measuring jug. Write down the amount of water your rain gauge has collected. Put the empty rain gauge back in its place to catch the next fall of rain. Keep a record of the amount of rain that falls each day during a week or a month.

Clouds can tell you whether it's likely to rain. Wispy, thin clouds high in the sky show that the weather will be fine for some time. Fluffy, white cumulus clouds like these on the right look like cotton wool. If there is a lot of blue sky between them, the weather will stay fine. But if the clouds grow bigger, there could be showers of rain.

Thick layers of clouds like these are called stratus. If the layers are heavy and grey, it means there will be rain which could last for hours.

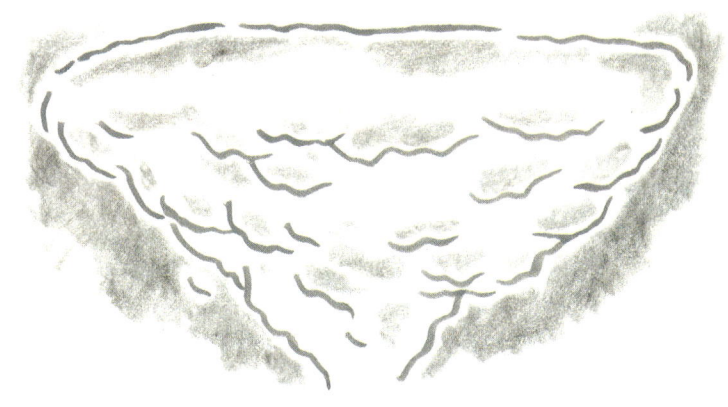

Huge grey cumulonimbus clouds like these can bring storms of rain, hail, thunder and lightning. You may see the clouds building up before the storm begins.

Make a weather diary

You can use your rain guage to help you make a weather diary. A weather diary will show how the weather in your area changes from day to day. Start by recording the amount of rainfall each day. Make a note of the temperature of the air outside – does it vary much from day to day?

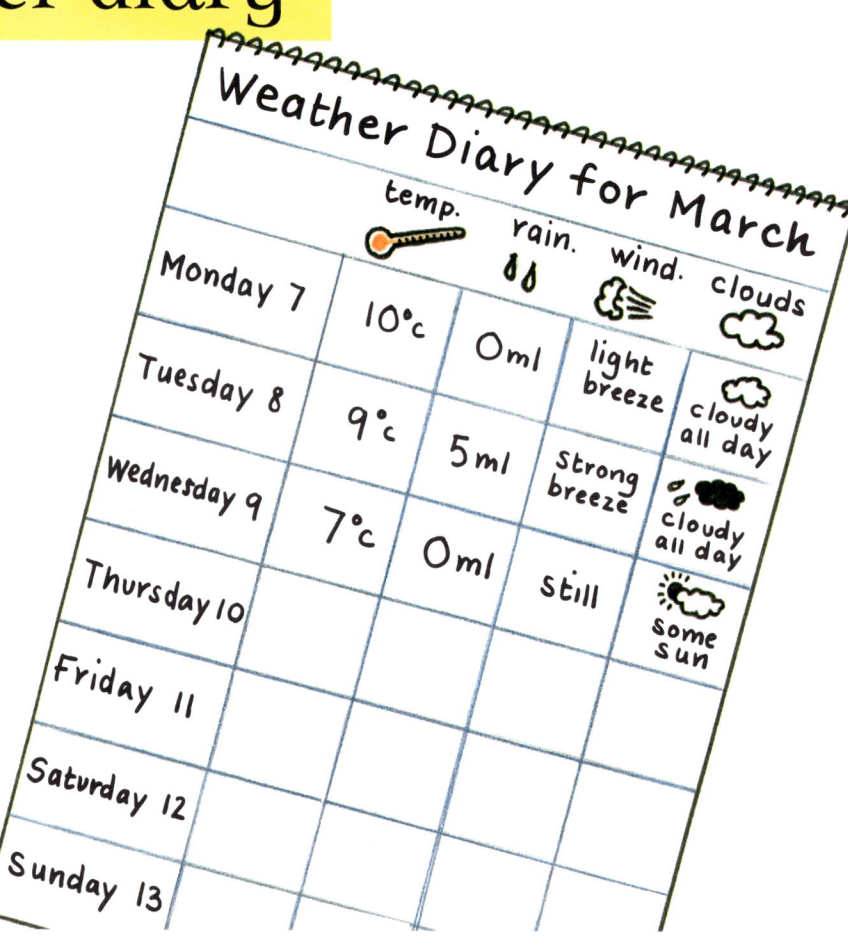

Weather Diary for March

	temp.	rain.	wind.	clouds
Monday 7	10°c	0ml	light breeze	cloudy
Tuesday 8	9°c	5ml	Strong breeze	cloudy all day
Wednesday 9	7°c	0ml	still	some sun
Thursday 10				
Friday 11				
Saturday 12				
Sunday 13				

How windy is it? You can find out by holding up a toy windmill to see how fast the sails whir round. You can tell in which direction the wind is blowing by making a simple windsock. Stretch a nylon stocking over a thin wire frame and attach the frame to a stick.

You can use your windsock to test the speed of the wind, too. If the sock hangs loosely when you hold it up in the air, it means that the windspeed is very low. If the sock stands straight out, the wind is blowing much faster.

Sometimes the wind blows so fast that it is dangerous. This picture was taken from a Space Shuttle above the clouds. It shows a huge storm called Hurricane Elena. The winds swirl towards the centre which is called the 'eye' of the storm. The speed of the wind in a hurricane can be as much as 360 kilometres an hour. Hurricanes can cause huge damage if they blow over land.

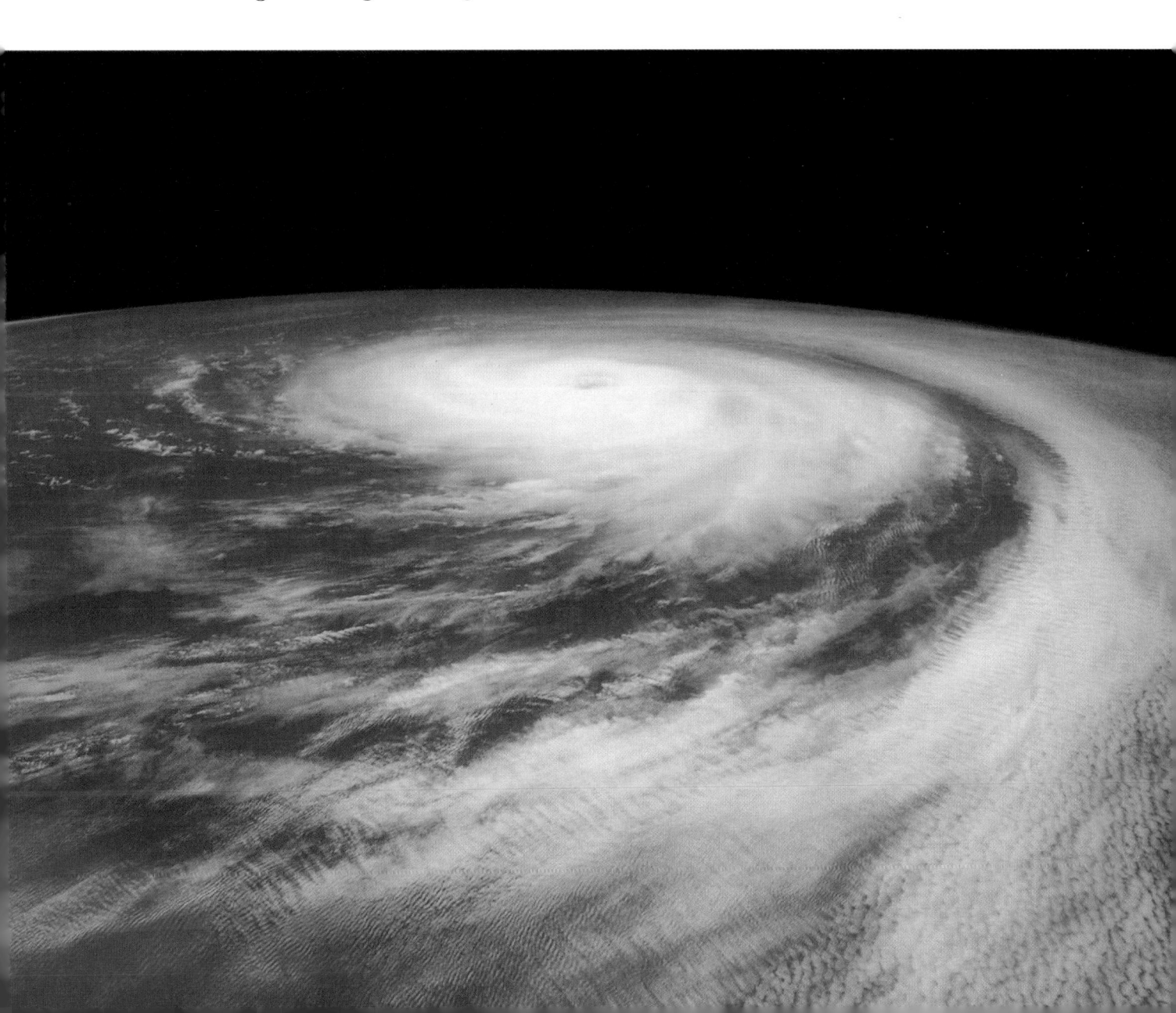

Notes for teachers and parents

As you share this book with children, these notes will help you to get the most from the investigations.

Why is the Sun so important? (pages 6, 7)

A black tray of water will absorb the Sun's energy more efficiently than a white or shiny one. Light coloured or reflective surfaces reflect away a large proportion of the solar radiation, absorbing only a small part of it. Dull black surfaces absorb radiation much more readily. It is important to shelter the tray from any wind, which will have a severe cooling effect on the water. If you do not have a suitable sunny day, an ordinary lamp shining on the tray will show the effect quite well.

What is gravity? (pages 8, 9)

A box weighing about 1kg and a lump of plasticene were used as the weights in this picture. Obviously great care should be taken not to drop the weights on to the onlookers! It is much easier to get the two weights to start falling together if only one person drops both. Given a fair start like this, and minimal air resistance, the weights will land at the same time. Listen for one thud or two thuds as they hit the ground.

Investigating rocks (pages 12, 13)

The growing of beautiful, large crystals takes time and care. A two-stage process is necessary, one to make tiny seed crystals, and the second to allow one of the seeds to grow larger in a saturated solution of the same chemical.

Salt is not the only crystal you can grow at home. Try sugar, or the beautiful blue rhomboid crystals of copper sulphate. For all these it is important to have slow undisturbed growth, which may take days or even weeks. The thread holding the seed crystal can be suspended from a pencil resting on the top of the jar.

NB Care should be taken if using copper sulphate with young children. It is toxic, and must not be put in the mouth.

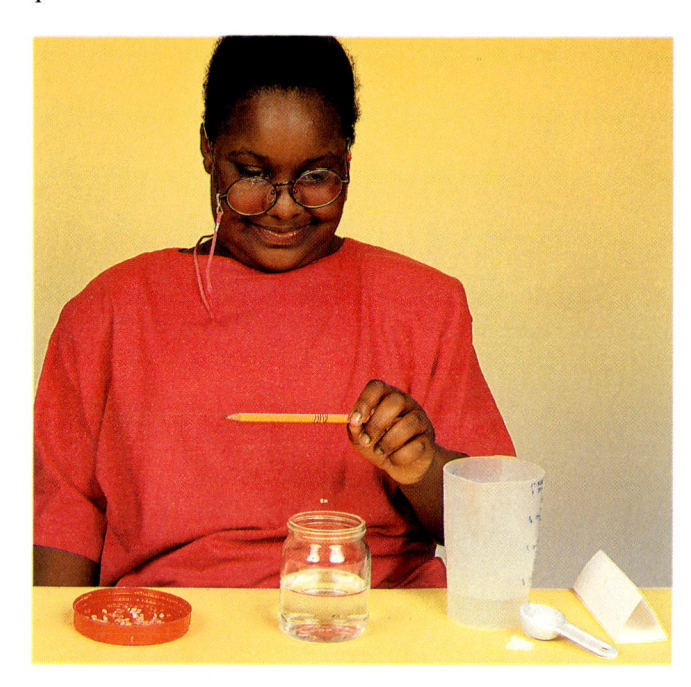

What are fossils? (pages 14, 15)

Always accompany children on their investigations of beaches, hills and quarries and ask for permission from the quarry owner before you make your visit.

Investigating soil (pages 16, 17)

A magnifying glass is not necessary to see the different layers of soil settling out of the water. However, it may be interesting to look closely at the particles in each layer.

24

The Earth's water supply (pages 18, 19)

The true gaseous form of water, water vapour, is invisible. It is only when it cools and forms tiny droplets that it looks white and cloudy. You can see this happening at the spout of a boiling kettle. The water vapour coming out of the spout is clear, but it becomes cloudy a few centimetres away. A demonstration of this may explain to the children why they cannot usually see the water vapour rising from the sea, but they can see it when it condenses into clouds.

Investigating rainfall (pages 20, 21)

The rain gauge could also be made from suitable kitchen equipment such as a funnel and a jar. The usual way to note the rainfall is to measure the DEPTH of water in the gauge, for which you could use a plastic ruler with cm and mm markings. However, plastic bottles have an uneven base and it may be much easier to measure the VOLUME of water by pouring it into a measuring jug, as shown in the photograph. Either method will give valuable practice in the skill of accurate measurement.

Make a weather diary (page 22, 23)

The form of the record sheet could be designed by the children. They should consider for themselves how to indicate sunshine, wind and cloud. This is an opportunity to introduce the weather symbols commonly used in forecasts.

The outside temperature will vary during the day, of course. Aim for the mid-afternoon temperature which will be around maximum for the day.

Index

air 4, 9, 19
America 8
animals 5, 7, 14, 16, 17
Apollo astronauts 3
Asia 8
atmosphere 4, 5
Australia 8

beaches 13, 14

chalk 16
clay 16, 17
cliffs 15
clouds 3, 19, 21
   cumulonimbus 21
   cumulus 21
   stratus 21
core 10
crust 11, 12
crystals 12, 13
curve of the Earth 2

dust 4

Earth's layers 10, 11
energy 6, 7
Europe 8
evaporation 19
Everest 11

fossils 14, 15

gas 4, 5
gemstone jewellery 12
granite 12
gravity 8, 9
grit 16, 17

heat 5, 6, 7, 19
human body 8, 19
humus 16, 17

iguana 7
iron 10

lakes 18, 19
lava 10
layers of the earth 10, 11
light 6
living things 5, 6, 19

magma 10, 12
mantle 10
Mercury 4
Moon 3, 5
mountains 11

nickel 10

oceans 3, 18
oxygen 5

pebbles 13
planets 2, 4
plants 6, 14, 16, 17, 19
power stations 7

quarries 15

rain gauge 20, 22
reptiles 15
rivers 14, 15, 18, 19
rock 3, 10, 12, 13, 14, 15, 16

sand 14, 16, 17
satellite 23
sea 14, 15, 18, 19
soil 14, 16, 17
solar energy 7
Space Shuttle 2, 23
Solar System 4
stones 16, 17
streams 18, 19
Sun 2, 4, 5, 6, 7, 8, 19
surface of the Moon 5

temperature on Earth 5, 22

ultra-violet rays 5

Venus 4
volcano 10

water 3, 5, 7, 18, 19, 20
water cycle 19
weather 16, 21, 22
   hail 21
   hurricane 23
   lightning 21
   rain 19, 20, 21, 22
   thunder 21
   wind 19, 22, 23
windsock 22
worms 17

x-rays 5